CANADA

Josef Hanus & John Hanus

Personal gift to:

From:

Pacific Ocean

The western shores of British Columbia are washed with the waters of the Pacific Ocean. This picture was taken from Wreck Beach.

English Bay

English Bay is a part of Burrard Inlet.

2

Vancouver

Vancouver, the third largest city in Canada, is an important part of the Pacific Rim. Greater Vancouver is home to over 1.5 million residents.

Vancouver Library

The new Vancouver Library is located on West Georgia Street, in downtown Vancouver.

3

Grouse Mountain

Grouse Mountain rises above North Vancouver. This part of the Coast Mountains is a popular destination for hikers and skiers.

Seymour Mountain

Mount Seymour Provincial Park is a part of North Vancouver. Rising above Indian Arm and Deep Cove, Mt. Seymour is a favorite destination for skiers.

4

Stanley Park

Totem Poles in Stanley Park are a memory to the Squamish First Nations. The park, with its 40 hectares of forest, beaches and trails, is one of the most visited parks in Greater Vancouver.

Burnaby Village

Home of numerous heritage buildings, Burnaby Village Museum is located in Deer Lake Park, in Burnaby.

5

Lynn Creek

Lynn Creek springs from the Coast Mountains, near Palisade Lake. The location of this photograph is in Lynn Valley, North Vancouver.

Harrison Lake

Harrison Hot Springs and Harrison Lake are a part of the Hemlock Valley, 120km from Vancouver.

British Columbia

Mount Robson

Mount Robson, part of the Rocky Mountains and the highest point in the Canadian Rockies, is located on the Alberta—British Columbia border.

Nelson

The heritage city of Nelson is located between Castlegar and Kootenay Lake.

British Columbia

Skeena River

The scenery in this picture is close to Terrace, in Kitsumkalum Provincial Park. Hwy #16, Prince George—Prince Rupert.

Mt. Pendleton

Traveling from Watson Lake, Yukon, over the Cassiar Highway to Dease Lake, you will see Mt. Pendleton just above Good Hope Lake.

8

British Columbia

Mt. Edith Cavell

Jasper National Park is the most popular park in Canada. Mt. Edith Cavell with its 3363 m, is located close to Jasper.

Angel Glacier

Angel Glacier is a part of Mt. Edith Cavell.

11

Alberta

Athabasca Glacier

Thousands of tourists visit Athabasca Glacier each day. Highway #93, Jasper–Banff

Columbia Icefield

Mount Athabasca and Columbia Icefield are located on the border of two parks, Jasper and Banff National Parks.

12

West Edmonton Mall

The size of 104 football fields, the mall holds the world's largest indoor lake, complete with submarines, a wave pool and the world's largest shopping centre, it's one of the most famous malls worldwide.

Edmonton

The capital city of Alberta. Edmonton, and the Saskatchewan River are the focus of this picture.

13

Dinosaur Park

Dinosaur Provincial Park, located by Highway 551, was established in 1955 and covers 90 square km.

Calgary

Alberta's "Sandstone City." After a big fire in 1886, log construction was prohibited in Calgary. Many buildings in downtown are built from yellow sandstone.

14

Alberta

Cypress Hills Park

Cypress Hills Provincial Park can be reached from Medicine Hat by Hwy. #1 and #48. Varied recreational activities attract many sports enthusiasts.

Medicine Hat

North America's circuit cowboys are attracted by Medicine Hat's July Exhibition and Stampede. Medicine Hat is located on Hwy. #1, 60km west of the Saskatchewan border.

15

Alberta

Banff National Park

This world-famous National Park is located in the Rocky Mountains.

Lake Louise

Lake Louise, located in Banff National Park just 30km northwest of Banff, is the most popular recreational area in Alberta.

16

Alberta

Waterfowl Lakes

Four million visitors each year visit Banff National Park, which was established in 1887.

Mount Amery

Banff National Park

17

Alberta

Cannington Manor

Several houses remain from the colony, established here in 1882 by English aristocrats. Cannington Manor Historic Park can be reached by Hwy #13 and #9.

Diefenbaker Lake

Douglas Provincial Park and Diefenbaker Lake are recreational facilities located 150km west of Moose Jaw along Hwy. #42.

Wheat Fields

Hard red spring wheat and Durum wheat are common Saskatchewan grains, grown mostly in southern Saskatchewan.

Regina

Regina, Saskatchewan's largest city, is also the capital city of this province. The subject of this picture is Regina's Legislative Building and Wascana Lake.

19

Saskatchewan

Saskatoon

Saskatoon is province's second largest city. This photograph of the city skyline was taken across the South Saskatchewan River.
The city is home to the University of Saskatchewan.

Fall Rye Field

This early morning spring picture of a Fall rye field was taken near Turtleford. Fall rye grain is used for flour and for distilling whiskey.

Qu Appelle Valley

Qu Appelle River Valley is located 70km north of Regina, by Hwy #11. The valley is well known for Saskatoon berries, pin cherries and black currants.

Donkey Head

Oil pumps can often be seen in Saskatchewan. This picture was taken near Estevan.

Cypress Hills

Cypress Hills Provincial park is an interprovincial park, located 30km south of Maple Creek. The eastern and western sections together are over 200 square kilometres.

Frenchman Valley

Frenchman River Valley is located near Eastend, by Hwy #13.

22

Saskatchewan

Alameda, silo

Wheat Pools—large silos, are an inseparable part of Saskatchewan's nature. This picture was taken in Alameda, in the southern part of Saskatchewan.

Rape seed field

Endless yellow fields of rape seed, the oil grain used for Canola oil, is seen everywhere in Saskatchewan.

23

Lake Winnipeg

Lake Winnipeg, 400km long and 100km wide, is larger than Lake Ontario. Picturesque places for summer sports Grand Beach, Hillside and Victoria beaches are located 100km north of Winnipeg.

Pine Falls

Waters from the Lake-of-the-Woods flow into Winnipeg Lake through six hydroelectric plants, turning Winnipeg River water rapids into electricity for Manitoba.

24

Manitoba

Winnipeg

The city of Winnipeg is the capital city of Manitoba.
Half of the Manitoban population lives in Winnipeg.

The Forks

The Forks National Historic Site, located close to the junction of the Assiniboine and Red Rivers, is a popular city recreational location.

25

Shilo

The Royal Regiment of Canadian Artillery Museum at CFB Shilo. The museum is located near Brandon and Carberry.

Spirit Sands

Spruce Woods Provincial Heritage Park, with its 250 square km is located near Carberry. Spirit Sands is a part of this park.

26

Swinging Bridge

Souris swinging bridge was first built in 1903. The bridge is 177m long and is Canada's longest free suspension bridge. Souris is known as the prettiest prairie town.

Virden

Virden is a small city with beautiful architecture. The city is located by the Trans-Canada Hwy, 80km west of Brandon.

27

Sunset near Minto

Fields of durum wheat, hard red spring wheat, fall rye and flax are seen everywhere around, traveling across Manitoba.

Silos near Brandon

28

Lake-of-the-Woods

Lake-of-the-Woods is situated by the border with Manitoba. The mining and paper-pulp town of Kenora, is the largest town on the Lake-of-the-Woods.

Sioux Narrows

Sioux Narrows Provincial Park and Whitefish Bay. The bridge across the bay is the world's longest single-span wooden bridge.

31

Sault Ste. Marie

Sault Ste. Marie is the second largest city in steel production. It is the location of an important canal in the St. Lawrence seaway system. This photo shows Roberta Bondar Park.

Sudbury, Walden

General view of Sudbury, the nickel mine city. Sudbury is located by the Trans-Canada Hwy, 390km west of Toronto.

32

Lake Ontario

This photograph of Lake Ontario, Toronto Inner Harbour, Conference Centre, Harbour Square and Gardiner Expressway was taken from the highest point of the CN Tower.

Downtown Toronto

Old city, Wellington Street, Chinatown, Yorkville, Nathan Phillips Square and Yonge Street attract strollers day and night.

35

Huron Lake

Sturgeon Bay Provincial Park, located on the shore of Georgian Bay, is a beautiful recreational area just by the Trans-Canada Hwy.

Massey

Massey is located by the Trans-Canada Hwy near Spanish River and Chutes Provincial Park. The view in this picture is Immaculate Conception Parish Church in Massey.

36

Ontario

Peterborough

Peterborough, located 150km east of Toronto, is an interesting place, with numerous examples of beautiful architecture; old buildings and churches. St.George United Church is in this picture.

Lift Lock

Peterborough hydraulic lift lock was opened in 1904. It is the largest hydraulic lock in the world.

37

Ottawa

Ottawa became the capital of Canada in 1857. The city is located in the very eastern part of Ontario, just on the border with Quebec.

Parliament Hill

Wellington Street is the site of the gothic Parliamentary buildings. Parliament Hill rises above the Ottawa River, which is the border with Hull, in Quebec.

38

Québec City

Standing majestically above the St. Lawrence River, Québec City is the capital of the province of Québec. Turreted Chateau Frontenac is shown, built in 1895.

St. Louis Street

Romantic downtown is full of art, small restaurants and heritage buildings. Québec is a city with a rich history, beginning in 1608, when Canada's oldest city was founded.

39

St. Lawrence River

This view of the St. Lawrence River, Champlain Blvd. and the ferry dock was taken from Dufferin Terrace.

Rivière-Trois-Pistoles

Rivière-Trois-Pistoles is located on the south shore of the St. Lawrence. The river is 20km wide here. Beautiful beaches and romantic villages are scattered along the shores of this river.

40

Montréal

Montréal is the second largest city in Canada, located on a 50km-long island in the St. Lawrence River. Montréal's harbour invites 3500 commercial boats annually.

Downtown Montréal

Montréal is a city of modern, expansive architecture.
Victoria Place Park and La tour de la Bourse are seen in this picture.

41

Québec

Rivière-du-Loup

Rivière-du Loup is the largest
community on the lower
St. Lawrence River, located in
the western part of Gaspé
Peninsula, by Hwy #20.

St-Cleophas

Scenery photo near St-Cleophas,
Gaspé Peninsula, Hwy #132.

42

Québec

Drummondville

Village Québecois d'Antan is the name of this village with 70 heritage houses, located by the Trans-Canada Hwy. Drummondville was settled by British veterans in 1815.

Matapedia River

Lac-au-Saumon is the point of this photo, located in the western part of the Gaspé Peninsula.

Saint John River

St. John River, photographed between Temple and Allande, by Trans-Canada Hwy 2.

Fredericton

Fredericton's City Hall was built in 1876. It is Atlantic Canada's oldest City Hall still in use. Fredericton, the capital of New Brunswick, was settled in 1783.

44

New Brunswick

Bay of Fundy

The Rocks Park, located 30km south of Moncton, is known for its extreme high and low tides. The Rocks Provincial Park and Hopewell Cape are the favored tourist destination, next to Fundy Nat'l Park, St.Martin Beach and Fundy Footpath, located on the shore of Chignecto Bay, which is a part of the Bay of Fundy.

Tree Farms

Tree Farms near Hammondvale.

45

New Brunswick

Moncton

Moncton is the second largest city in New Brunswick, and an important industrial and cultural centre. Université de Moncton is the only french language university located east of Québec. Downtown places of historical interest include Moncton Civic Museum, Free Meeting House, the Capital Theatre and Acadian Museum.

46

Parlée Beach

Parlée Beach is one of many beautiful beaches located on the shore of Northumberland Strait and the Gulf of St. Lawrence. The beaches east of Moncton are known as "Florida North."

Robichaud

Fishing wharf Robichaud is located near Cap Pélé and Murray Beach Provincial Park, on the shore of Northumberland Strait.

Saint John

Saint John, the largest city in New Brunswick, founded in 1783, is the oldest incorporated city in Canada. Located on the shore of the Bay of Fundy, it is an important sea port.

Saint John Harbour

Downtown Saint John was photographed across the Saint John harbour, from the pier.

48

Magnetic Hill

A fascinating tourist and motorist attraction, Magnetic Hill, was first popularized in 1933. The road appears to be going uphill, but the opposite is true. Motorists can check out this illusion, coasting uphill in neutral.

Edmundston

Industrial, pulp producing city on the junction of St. John and Madawaska Rivers, just on the state boundary with Maine.

49

Halifax

Halifax, the capital city of Nova Scotia and the biggest city in Atlantic Canada, was founded in 1794. This picture was taken from Halifax Citadel. At the Halifax cemetery, there are many graves for the victims of the Titanic.

Halifax Harbour

Halifax Harbour is one of world's largest harbours, inviting 3500 vessels every year from around world. Munition ship Mont Blanc exploded here in 1917 with extreme force.

50

Lunenburg

Located between Mahone Bay and Lunenburg Harbour, just 80km west of Peggy's Cove, Lunenburg is another beautiful tourist spot along the Atlantic Ocean.
The port was settled in 1780 by Swiss, German and French immigrants. Colorful 'Old Town' Lunenburg is a Unesco World Heritage Site, home port of the Bluenose II schooner, and the Fisheries Museum.

53

Ingonish Beach

Cape Breton Highlands National Park is located in northern Nova Scotia, Cape Breton Island. Ingonish Beach and Ingonish resort are beautiful recreational centres on the eastern part of the Cabot Trail.

Cape Smoky

A view from Ingonish to Cape Smoky and the Atlantic Ocean.

Cabot Trail

The 300km trip around Cape Breton is a breathtaking tourist trail named after John Cabot, who first climbed the hilly and sandy terrain of the islands shores in 1497. Cabot Trail is one of the most popular tourist trails in North America. This shot of the western part of Cabot Trail was taken by Pleasant Bay, close to Cap Rouge.

Inverness

Fishing village by Cabot Trail.

55

St. George's Bay

Cape Breton Island is separated
from the mainland by the Strait
of Canso, a part of George Bay.
The view of this bay was taken
from Cape George.

Wreck Cove

This beautiful view of the
Cabot Trail can be found
above Wreck Cove.

56

Confederation Bridge

The Link, a 13km long bridge, is the world's longest multispan bridge. Completed in May 1997, the bridge connects Prince Edward Island with the mainland of Canada, bringing to P.E.I. thousands of tourists from around the world and providing year-round commercial transport across the ice-covered waters of Northumberland Strait.

57

Borden-Carleton

Sunset along a sandbank near Borden Carleton, close to the Confederation Bridge, on the shore of Northumberland Strait.

Beaches of P.E.I.

Beautiful beaches surround the Island. This photograph was taken near Stanhope, Prince Edward Island National Park.

58

Charlottetown

Charlottetown, the capital of Prince Edward Island, is the smallest provincial capital and the only city in this province. Charlottetown was settled by the British in 1764, and is the birth place of Canada. In September 1864, the first meeting of the Canadian Confederation took place here. This picture of the city was taken in front of the Government House.

59

Victoria

The Fishing wharf of Victoria, near Hampton, Trans-Canada Hwy #1.

Tryon

Tryon and Tryon River, a village near Crapaud, Trans-Canada Hwy #1.

Green Gables

Cavendish is home to Green Gables and the movie location of Lucy Maud Montgomery's famous novel, *Anne of Green Gables*.

Murray Harbour

Murray River and Murray Harbour, a fishing village near the Fantasyland Provincial Park.

61

St. Mary's Bay

The shore of the Atlantic ocean in St. Mary's is a place of final rest for the first, original, European settlers in Newfoundland. Some of them were born as early as 1668.

Atlantic Ocean

Cape Spear is located several kilometres from St. John's. The cape, with a beautiful view of the Atlantic is the easternmost point of Canada. Many tourists come here to see whales, the lighthouse, and to visit an old World War II bunker.

St. John's

St. John's, the capital city of Newfoundland, is a city of contrast; you will find modern architecture, next to the oldest streets in North America. The city is located on east side of the island.

Signal Hill Park

Signal Hill with the Cabot Tower rises 150m above the entrance to St. John's Harbour. The tower was built in memory of Cabot's discovery of Newfoundland in 1497.

63

Petty Harbour

Avalon Peninsula is the eastern-most part of Newfoundland. Close to St. John's in Cochrane Pond Prov. Park, the small fishing village of Petty Harbour is nestled in one of numerous romantic coves in Shoal Bay. The pictures show Petty Harbour's St. George Anglican Church and a still life shot from the village. Three km east of Petty Harbour is Cape Spear, the eastern-most point in Canada. *(see p. 62)*

St. John's Harbour

First settlers built their houses around Newfoundland's bays around 1500. John Cabot moored his vessel in 1497. In 1583, the island was claimed for Queen Elizabeth. In 1665, the French and Dutch burned and plundered the town. In 1762, the British regained the town, which was destroyed in 1892 by fire, and rebuilt again. The pictures show the entrance to the harbour and Fort Amherst.

65

Bonne Bay

Bonne Bay and Lobster Cove is the focus of this sunset picture. The northern peninsula is the location of Gros Morne National Park, which is the most visited park in Newfoundland. It is named for the island's second highest peak, Gros Morne, 806 m. *(page 67)*

Rocky Harbour

Rocky Harbour fishing village, in Gros Morne National Park.

Lobster Cove Head

"Lobster Cove Head" Lighthouse is situated on the rocks above Bonne Bay, in Gros Morne Prov. Park. Surrounded by a tourist park, there is a wide view of the gulf of St. Lawrence and Bonne Bay.

Gros Morne

Second highest peak in Newfoundland, Gros Morne is a part of the Long Range Mountains, which form the Northern peninsula.

67

Margaree, Fox Roost

The fishing village of Margaree is situated several miles east from Port-aux-Basques Channel, a ferry port to Sydney, Nova Scotia. Cabot Strait separates Newfoundland from Nova Scotia. A modern car and passenger ferry takes about 6 hours to reach North Sydney from the west part of Newfoundland. A ferry from Argentia on the Avalon Peninsula, close to St. John's, takes 15 hrs to reach the shores of Nova Scotia.

New World Island

The fishing village of Twillingate is situated on New World Island in the Bay of Exploits. A beautiful 100km long trip, north from Gander by Hwy #1 through Jonathan's and Dildo Run Provincial Parks by Hwy. 330 and numerous romantic fishing villages ends at Twillingate and Durrell.

Durrell

A fishing village located in Wild Cove, close to Gillesport, Hwy. 340.

69

Diable Bay

Newfoundland's Labrador region can be reached by ferry from Black Duck Cove, located in the northern part of Northern Peninsula, Hwy 430. The ferry connects Blanc Sablon from the spring to late fall. Labrador can be reached by car from Baie Comeau, Québec, or by airplane. The photographs show Diable Bay and Pinware River, both located in the Strait of Belle Isle, 70km from the ferry port in Blanc Sablon.

70

South Nahanni

Fall colours on the South Nahanni River, located between Nahanni Range and Tlogotsho Range, close to Hwy #7.

Richardson Mountains

Located on the border with the Yukon close to Fort McPherson, 150km south of Inuvik by the Dempster Hwy.

S.S. Klondike

Whitehorse, the capital of the Yukon, is situated near Kluane National Park on the Alaska Highway. It is the largest city in the Yukon, settled in 1898. The S.S. Klondike, the last sternwheeler operated on the Yukon River, is kept in Whitehorse as a transport museum.

Five Finger Rapids

The Yukon River is divided into five streams by high sandstone columns. The rapids are located 150km north of Whitehorse, via Klondike Hwy.

74

Champagne

Yukon Plateau and Miners Range
is the location of this fall picture.
Close to Champagne, which was a
post of the Northwest Mounted
Police on the Dalton Trail by
Alaska Hwy.

Moose

Moose and Caribou can be seen
everywhere in the southern Yukon,
very often by the highways. It is
nice to see them by daylight, but
very dangerous to encounter them
while driving at night.

75

Jack London's Cabin

Jack London, the famous writer of the North and the Gold Rush is very closely connected to Dawson City. His cabin is still here on Eighth Ave close to Klondike and Yukon Rivers.

Dawson City

Arriving for the first time via the Klondike Highway to a nighttime Dawson City, and seeing the Northern Lights on the black sky is an unforgettable moment. Dawson City is a beautiful and romantic place in Canada's north.

76

Tintina Trench

Mountains above Dawson City.

Yukon River

The Yukon River flows from Atlin Lake. Passing through Whitehorse to Dawson City and then through Alaska, it empties into the Pacific Ocean. Its journey is over 1500km long. Our picture of the Yukon River is from Dawson City, where a ferry connects the Klondike highway and the Top of the World Hwy, toward Alaska.

77

Dempster Highway

The 780km long Dempster Highway connects Inuvik with Dawson City and Whitehorse, through summer and winter. Beginning 30km east of Dawson City, Dempster Hwy winds through charming mountain scenery, around beautiful rivers and unending plains. Shortly after Eagle Plains it passes the Arctic Circle and reveals a breathtaking view of the Richardson Mountains. After Fort McPherson, the highway passes over tundra to Inuvik, Northwest Territories.

Yukon

Top of the World

Across the Yukon River in Dawson City, the Klondike Highway is named "Top of the World Highway." For the next 70km, to the border with Alaska, the highway winds along the ridge of the Klondike Plateau. In the fall, the mountains change to amazing red and yellow colors.

Klondike Plateau

Arctic Circle

Eagle Plains is the first post after driving over the Dempster Hwy, a distance of 500km from Dawson City. The Arctic Circle and Eagle Plains are surrounded by the beautiful Richardson Mountains. Thirty kilometers past Eagle Plains is the Arctic Circle. Another 270km further, through the Richardson Mountains, and then over tundra, is Inuvik. Driving over the Dempster Highway, was the most beautiful trip of my life. —*JH*

80